My Daddy Is In Jail

Story, Discussion Guide, &

Small Group Activities For Grades K–5

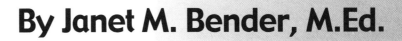

By Janet M. Bender, M.Ed.

© 2013, 2012, 2010, 2008, 2007, 2005, 2003
YouthLight, Inc.
Chapin, SC 29036

ISBN 978-1-889636-48-1

Library of Congress Number: 2002114045

10 9 8 7
Printed in the United States

PO Box 115
Chapin, SC 29036
800-209-9774
803-345-1070
803-345-0888 fax
yl@youthlightbooks.com
www.youthlightbooks.com

Dedication

This book is dedicated to all the innocent children whose lives are impacted by the incarceration of a parent or loved one.

Acknowledgements

I thank the dozens of children who have taught me so much by sharing their thoughts, feelings and art work with me.

A special thanks to Ashlyn Howard for her assistance with some of the drawings.

Table Of Contents

Introduction

Over the past twenty years as an elementary school counselor, I have come in contact with many children who were struggling to cope with their feelings about having an incarcerated parent. Finding no resources in the school media center to draw from, I decided to listen to the children and help them put their feelings into words. This story, discussion and small group activity guide, is the culmination of many sessions with elementary children who trusted me with their private thoughts and feelings. I have worked with these children both individually and in small groups.

The first section of this book provides statistics and helpful information about incarcerated parents and their children. The next section offers suggestions for using this book with children and their caregivers. The children's story with discussion questions comes next, followed by the optional small group activities.

It is my hope that this book will serve as bibliotherapy in the hands of caring adults to help relieve a little of the burden these children carry while affirming their innate self-worth.

Janet M. Bender

Why Is This Resource Needed?

Although there has been very little research done with these children and their caregivers, a review of publications on parents in jail presents disturbing predictions about the profound effects of parental incarceration on children. In the studies that do exist, it is evident that the estimated 1.5 million children in the U. S. with parents who are incarcerated "have experienced disrupted and multiple placements, decreased quality of care, financial hardship, and lack of contact with the parents. Consequently, these children are at risk for poor academic achievement, substance abuse, delinquency, and future incarceration." (Seymour)

We know that parental imprisonment results in extreme stress similar to that felt by children who experience loss through death, divorce, or trauma. In his paper, *Counseling Children Who Have Experienced Extreme Stressors,* Alexander Leon considers the possibility of utilizing the school community as a therapeutic support system for these children.*

Specifically, these children are "vulnerable to feelings of fear, anxiety, anger, sadness, depression and guilt." The social stigma and tendency to identify with their incarcerated parents, may cause their self esteem and social interaction skills to suffer, often producing "behavioral consequences such as emotional withdrawal, failure in school, and delinquency." (Simmons)

Another concern is the children's limited contact with incarcerated parents and the quality of substitute care given to these children due to multiple and sometimes questionable placements. Children with parents in jail usually receive care from foster parents or extended family members. In a study on substitute care for children of incarcerated mothers, the quality of substitute care from foster families for 3-6 year old children was found to be significantly better than care from relatives, but equal for infants and toddlers. (Gaudin & Sutphen)

Perhaps the most disturbing discovery is that very little is being done to address the needs of children of arrested parents. We know that these children are at high risk for a number of negative behaviors, but the lack of research and official policy on the matter means that these children and their caregivers are seldom targeted for treatment or support services. (Simmons)

A recent survey of inmates in state and federal correctional facilities revealed the following alarming statistics regarding incarcerated parents and their children. The fact that these numbers continue to increase, indicates a need for societal action toward identifying and serving the needs of this population.

9

What We Know About Incarcerated Parents And Their Children

A Bureau of Justice Statistics report published in August 2000 by the U. S. Department of Justice revealed the following information:

- An estimated 336,300 U.S. households with minor children were affected by the incarceration of a resident parent.

- 32% of all state and federal prisoners reported having multiple minor children.

- 22% of all minor children with a parent in prison were under 5 years of age.

- 58% of the minor children were under 10 years of age and the average age of these children was 8 years old.

- An estimated 1.5 million children in the U. S. had a parent in prison—a 500,000 increase since 1991.

- During the 1990s, the number of children with a mother in prison has nearly doubled (up 98%) while the number of children with a father in prison increased by 58%.

- Almost 60% of the parents in state prisons reported having used drugs in the month before their offense, and 25% reported a history of alcohol dependence. More than a third of parents in state prisons committed their offense while under the influence of alcohol.

- 70% of parents in prison did not have a high school diploma.

- In the month before their arrest, 62% of imprisoned parents lived apart from their children.

How We Can Help

Within the school and the community, professional helpers, psychologists, social workers, parents, nurses, and other caring adults can help children develop positive coping skills to deal with family changes such as incarceration of a loved one. We can provide a supportive climate in which these children may process their grief, establish caring relationships, release shame, and build healthy self esteem. We, as caring adults, can communicate openly and empathetically with the children and their caregivers.

How To Use This Book

The children's story within this book may be used by itself or as a part of several small group counseling sessions.

Talking with young children about the issue of incarceration is extremely difficult. Children may experience feelings of fear, anger, shame, loss, confusion, loneliness and/or betrayal. These stressful feelings are often compounded by a climate of secrecy that may surround these situations. It is especially important to establish rapport and trust with the child and with the custodial parent/caregiver before seeking permission to place the child in a support group.

Counselors, parents, and other caring adults can use this story to encourage the child to express his/her feelings openly in a safe environment. It is important to avoid making judgments about the family or the incarcerated person. Respecting the family's right to confidentiality may prevent bringing undue stigma and embarrassment to the child.

As children move through the discussion questions and/or group activities, they should be allowed to express and process their mixed feelings toward the incarcerated individual. With your support, they will be able to retain a positive self-image in spite of their current family situation.

This story is designed to be read by an adult to a child or a small group of children. The facilitator's instructions, questions, and small group activities are provided as suggestions to use as needed. I recommend having drawing paper and crayons available where indicated to give children opportunities for expression through art.

Be flexible. Depending on the number and age of children, the amount of discussion generated, and time restrictions, the story may be read in one session or divided over several sessions. Group activities may be done along with reading the story, or the entire story may be presented in session two and referred back to as needed.

The story you are about to read depicts a young girl whose father goes to jail. It should be noted that incarceration may impact a child through mother or father, other relatives, siblings, friends or acquaintances. Your discussion of the story should be adapted to address these situations. Even though his/her experience may include different characters, the feelings addressed will be similar. The checklist just before the children's story may be duplicated to help you determine the extent of the child's experience with incarceration. You may be surprised to discover that his/her experience extends beyond the incident you know about. The following suggestions for care-givers may be duplicated and sent home with the child.

Suggestions For Caregivers Or Family Members Of Children Impacted By Incarceration

1. Provide quality time with the remaining parent, when possible, and other family members and friends. Don't isolate the family from normal interactions with others.

2. Protect younger children from all the frightful details. Be honest, but age-appropriate when explaining the cause for the incarceration.

3. Reassure the child that he/she will be taken care of in the absence of the incarcerated parent.

4. Continue with your normal routine and consistent discipline as much as possible.

5. Provide opportunities for discussion and decision-making. Use the experience to teach the child about the consequences of our choices and taking responsibility for our behaviors.

6. Avoid either "running down" or glorifying the person who is in jail. Simple, honest facts are best.

7. Always be aware that a child's self-esteem is closely interwoven with his/her image of his/her parents. What he/she hears about them will greatly effect the way the child feels about him/herself as an offspring of those parents.

8. Assist the child in maintaining communication with parent through calls, letters or visits whenever possible and prudent.

9. Remember, if handled sensitively, this experience can strengthen the child. It doesn't have to ruin a child's life.

Who do you know who has been arrested or gone to jail?

- ☐ MY DAD
- ☐ MY STEP DAD
- ☐ MY MOM
- ☐ MY STEP MOM
- ☐ MY BROTHER/SISTER
- ☐ MY UNCLE/AUNT
- ☐ MY GRANDPARENT
- ☐ SOMEONE ELSE _____

Draw a picture of that person in this box.

My Daddy Is In Jail

By Janet M. Bender, M.Ed.

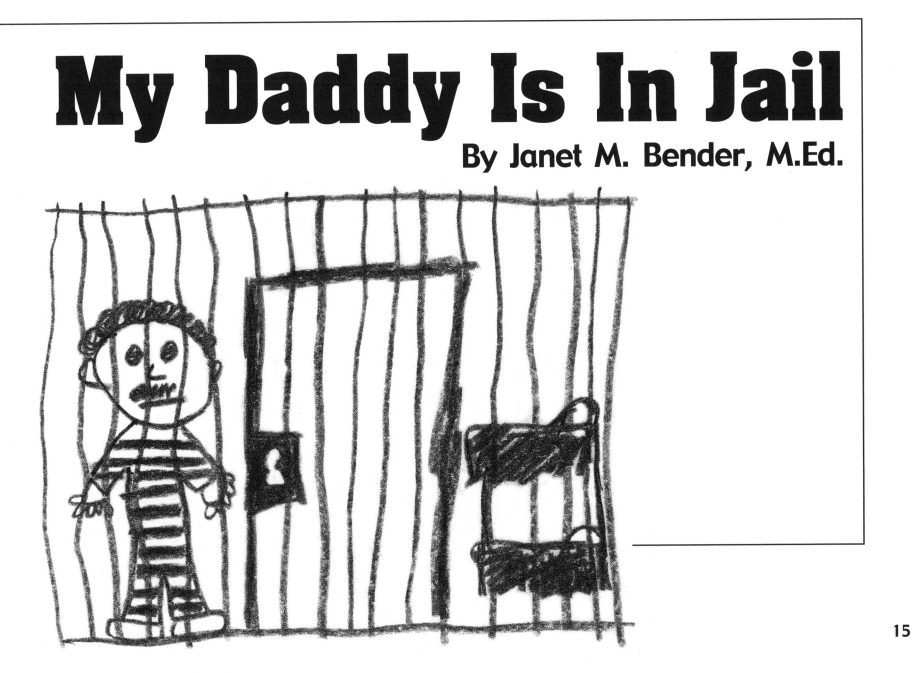

Discussion Guide

(Have drawing paper and crayons available in either loose leaf form or stapled in a booklet for each child to use throughout the group.)

Questions for discussion with story page 17:	Facilitator Comments:
1. How is Deena feeling? Why?	Living in prison or jail is very different from living in your home. In jail, people all wear the same kind of clothes called uniforms. They sleep on small bunk beds in a cell with bars and a locked door or gate. They cannot come and go places outside of the jail. They have guards to tell them what to do and where to go. Jails have tall fences or walls around them to keep people inside. What else do you know about jails?
2. Do you know of anyone who has gone to jail?	
3. Tell about or draw a picture to show how you feel.	
4. Have you ever seen a real jail or prison, or seen one on TV?	
5. How was it different from a home? *(small cells, bunk beds, bars and locks, lots of people, etc.)*	
6. What, if anything, scares you when you think about the person you know being in jail?	

Hi, my name is Deena.

My dad is in jail and I feel sad.

I don't understand much
about jail. I wonder about
a lot of things.

What is jail like?
Is it dirty?
Is it a scary place?

Discussion Guide

**Questions for discussion
with story page 19:**

1. What do you worry about?

2. When do you feel afraid?

3. What helps you feel better?

Sometimes I worry
about my dad.

Is he safe?
Is he sad too?

Sometimes I feel
scared, too.

Do you?

At night when I go
to bed, I sometimes
have bad dreams.
Mommy lets my
kitten sleep with
me. I pretend he
is a brave tiger
protecting me.
Then I feel safe.

Discussion Guide

**Questions for discussion
with story page 21:**

1. How did you first learn about
   your loved one going to jail?

2. What do you remember seeing,
   hearing, feeling, at that time?

I remember the day my Daddy left.

When I came home from school, I saw a police car in front of my house. I wondered what it was doing there.

I felt confused.

When I went inside, two policemen were putting handcuffs on my daddy. My mom was crying. She told me to go to my room.

21

Discussion Guide

**Question for discussion
with story page 23:**

1. Why do you think Deena
   tried not to cry?

   *(trying to be brave, maybe she
   thought it was not OK to show
   her sad feelings, especially
   for boys.)*

*I didn't want to go to my room.
I didn't want to be left alone.*

*But my mom was pretty upset,
so I went. I felt lonely. I hugged
my stuffed bear real tight and
tried to pretend that everything
was all right. I tried not to cry.*

*When I looked out my window,
I saw the police car drive away.*

*My daddy was gone.
I cried and cried.*

Discussion Guide

**Questions for discussion
with story page 25:**

1. Did you ever worry about
going to jail?

2. Do little children go to jail?

   (No, sometimes adults may threaten
   children to get them to follow the
   rules. Sometimes adults may say
   things they don't really believe
   when they are angry or upset.)

Everyone gets angry sometimes.

It's OK to feel angry. It can be

confusing when someone you love

gets angry with you and says or

does something that scares you.

3. Has that ever happened to you?
   Tell or draw about it.

4. When do you feel angry? Afraid?

5. What can you do to stay safe when
a grownup you know is angry?

   (Keep your distance, go to your
   room, obey rules, avoid talking
   back, etc.)

**Facilitator
Comments:**

It's OK to get your angry feelings

out in ways that do not:

1. **Hurt yourself**

2. **Hurt others**

3. **Damage or destroy property**

(Take some time to explore OK and
not Ok ways to express angry feelings.)

Later Mommy told me that daddy had
gone to jail because he broke the law.

I wondered, "If I am bad, will I go to jail too?"

Mommy doesn't want me to tell my friends about daddy being in jail.

It's hard keeping a big secret like this.
Sometimes I get mad at my mommy for making me keep a secret. Sometimes
I feel mad at my daddy for getting into trouble and going away.

Discussion Guide

Questions for discussion with story page 27:

1. What was it like at your house before your family member went to jail?

2. What is it like now?

3. What do you miss the most about the way it used to be?

Draw a picture of a fun time you remember having with your family member or friend who is in jail.

I think about the things my daddy used to do with me.

I miss playing with my daddy and having him tuck me in at night.

I wonder if he misses me too.

Discussion Guide

**Questions for discussion
with story pages 29 & 31:**

1. Do you ever visit _____ in jail?

2. If so, what is it like? If not, how do
   you feel about that?

Sometimes we have mixed feelings—

some good ones and some not so good

ones all mixed together. I call those

"scrambled eggs" feelings.

3. Do you ever have "scrambled eggs"
   feelings? Draw about them.

One Sunday a month,
Mommy takes me to
visit my dad.

Daddy seems different there.

I would like to ask my
daddy how he feels, but
I'm afraid he will get mad.
Sometimes daddy gets mad
at me when I ask him things.

I feel confused.

29

*My feelings seem
all mixed up.*

31

Discussion Guide

**Questions for discussion
with story page 33:**

1. Do you think your family member
   will come home again?

2. Who is taking care of you now?

3. Who will always take care of you?

I don't know if my daddy will come home again.

I would like to ask mommy about it, but I'm afraid she will get upset again. She cries whenever anyone talks about daddy.

If daddy doesn't come home, who will take care of Mommy and me?

Discussion Guide

**Questions for discussion
with story page 35:**

1. What things are the same as
   before your parent went to jail?

2. How are things/events different
   since your parent has been away?

On my birthday, we had cake and ice cream with my grandma and grandpa.

They gave me lots of nice presents, but nobody laughed and had fun like we used to.

Grandma told mommy that I seemed sad, and that I might need someone to talk to.

Discussion Guide

1. Who are some people you trust that
   you can talk to about your feelings?

   *(counselor, parent, teacher, pastor,
   friend, relative, social worker, foster
   parent, etc.)*

2. Is it your fault that your
   parent is in jail?

   *(No, you are only responsible for
   your own behavior.)*

The next week, Mommy talked with my teacher at school.

My teacher let me visit with the school counselor. Now I am in a sharing group with other boys and girls who have a parent in jail.

In group, I learned that all of my feelings are O.K. I don't have to pretend or hide my sad feelings anymore.

It feels good to know that I'm not a bad person because of what happened to my family.

It wasn't my fault.

Discussion Guide

(Have drawing paper and crayons available in either loose leaf form or stapled in a booklet for each child to use throughout the group.)

Questions for discussion with story page 39:	Facilitator Comments:
1. What will it be like if your family member comes home?	**The girl in the story wanted her Dad to come home again. Do all children feel that way?** (not necessarily)
2. What will it be like if he/she doesn't?	
3. Can you be safe and happy even if that person doesn't come home?	**Why?** (If the home was a scary place with that parent at home, it would be OK for the child to want things to be different.)
(Yes. Even though you may or may not like the way things turn out, you will be taken care of and you can choose to be happy again.)	

I hope Daddy does come home some day.

I hope things will be better.

I want to feel happy.

I want my family together again.

Optional Small Group Activities
For Use With Story

Objectives:

1. To express and process one's feelings about having a parent or loved one in prison.

2. To meet and share with other children in similar circumstances.

3. To strengthen one's self-esteem.

4. To share concerns and gain strategies for coping with them.

Session #1

Introductions & Goal Setting

Icebreaker such as the Name Game

Each student says his/her first name and a food he/she likes. i.e. "I'm Susie and I like spaghetti."

Group Rules

1) Take turns talking
2) Listen and make eye contact with speaker
3) No "put downs" / we're here to help each other
4) Option to pass
5) Confidentiality

Sharing Time

Introduce self and family with small people figures. Provide a container of people figures and take turns letting each child choose the ones that represent their family members. Discuss which members live where as they are introduced. After all have had a turn, help children identify a common theme. (They all come from families where someone is incarcerated.)

Goal Setting (See objectives)

Success Cards

Let group choose a success card* to record their attendance each week by placing a sticker on it. (A success card can be any picture with boxes on it for placing stickers.) Each session should end with the routine of getting stickers and whatever gesture of closure (handshake, hug, etc.) you have determined to use.

Enlarge and duplicate success cards on colorful card stock, or construction paper if available. Let students cut them out and display on the wall in your guidance office and take home at the end of group sessions.

*Success Card idea adapted from *Child Support Through Small Group Counseling,* 1984. L.Landy. KIDSRIGHTS

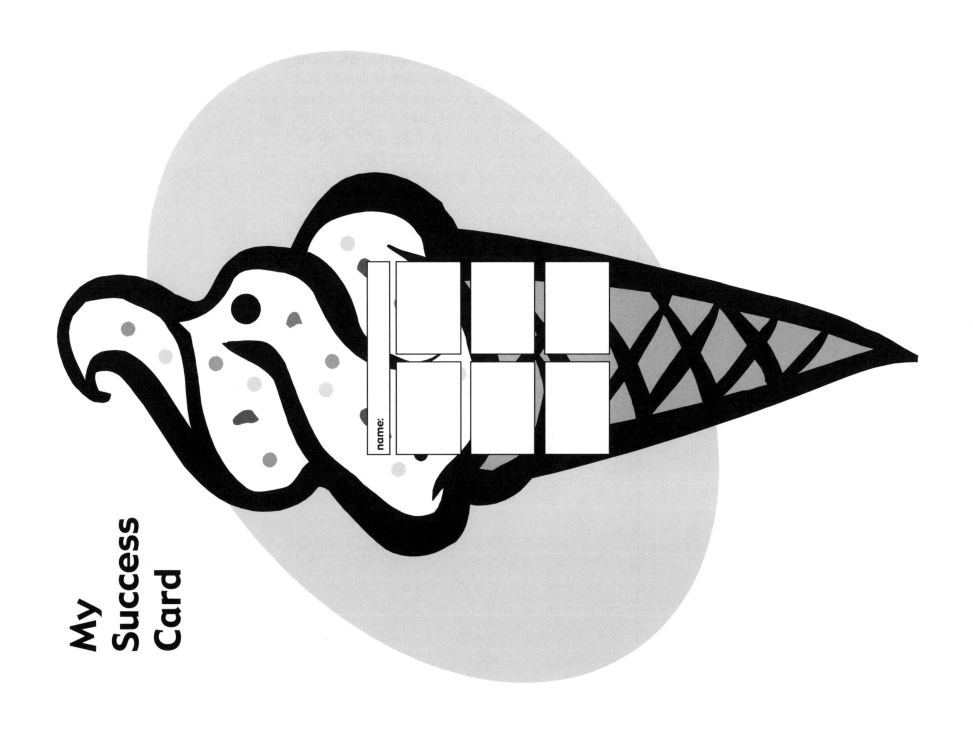

name:

My Success Card

Session #2

Scribble Your Feelings

(Heegaard)

Icebreaker such as the Name Game

Give each child a booklet of 10-12 blank sheets of drawing paper stapled together. Ask them to write their names on the front of the booklet. Explain to the students that usually in school they are expected to do their best work, but today and sometimes in this group, they will be allowed to draw however they feel. Have them open to the first page of their booklets. Provide a tub of crayons. Tell them you want them to do their worst work. Set a timer for 1 minute, and direct students to make the ugliest picture they can make in the time allowed. When time is up, let group vote on the ugliest picture.

Story

Introduce and begin reading story, **My Daddy is in Jail.**

Read story pages 17-21 and discuss.

Use drawing booklets each time students are asked to draw a picture.

Session #3

Expressing Feelings

Icebreaker such as the Name Game

Play "Guess the Feeling on My Face." Turn your back to the child/ren. Tell them that when you count to three with them, you will turn around and show a feeling on your face. They are to quickly call out the feeling expressed. (Show happy, sad, mad, scared, etc.)

Story

Read story pages 23-25.

Discuss and draw in booklets as suggested.

Feeling Monsters

After sharing OK and not OK ways to express angry feelings, give each student some clay or Play Doh and let them pound, squeeze, and poke it. Then direct them to create a "feeling monster" to match whatever feeling they want—angry, confused or scared. Let each share their monsters and tell how it feels and why.

Session #4

Worry Bees

(pattern included)

Discussion

Ask students what a rule is and why
we have rules *(for order and safety)*.

Discuss what consequences happen when
they break rules at school or at home.

Story

Read and discus story pages 27-31.

Follow-Up

Give each child a bee or let older children make a bee.
Ask them to give their worries to the worry bee by telling
him or writing on his wings about their worries.
(Leader can write for younger children as they dictate.)

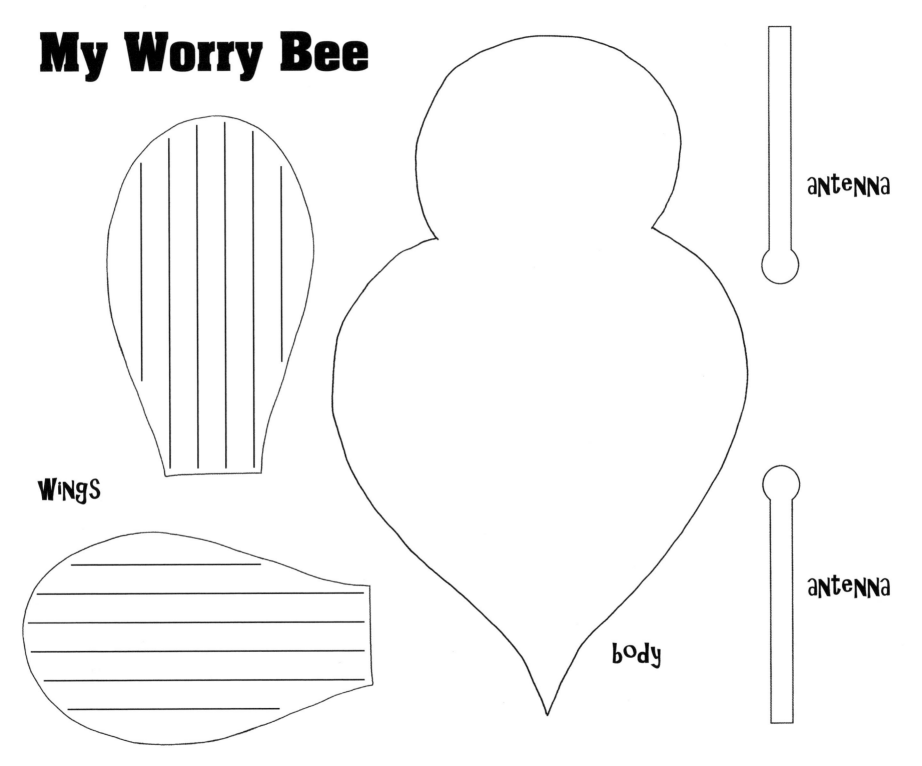

My Worry Bee

wings

antenna

antenna

body

Session #5

My Wishes

Sharing Time

Ask students if they have "imagination."

Discuss "imagination" and the difference between make-believe and real (what you wish versus what really is).

Then provide a container of small plastic animals and have each child choose one that s/he would like to be for a day. While pretending, ask children why they would want to be this animal. Validate feelings expressed.

Story

Read and discuss story pages 33-39.

Wishing Wand

Give each child a turn to hold the wand and make a wish. Make sure to explain to them that some wishes come true and some do not. Some things they can make happen like learning to write their name, and some things they have no control over, like how a friend acts.

Session #6

I'm Special

Name Game

Play the name game again, but this time ask each child to say his/her name and something special about him/herself. i.e. "I'm Janet and I can jump rope."

Sometimes it helps for the leader to start the game. If they have trouble thinking of answers, have them look in a mirror and tell something they see that they like, tell something they can do now that they couldn't do last year, or tell about a hobby or talent they have.

Art Activity

Provide drawing paper, scissors, crayons or markers, glue, old magazines, and a variety of decorative stickers. Ask each child to make a collage mini-poster that shows things they like.

Discuss the uniqueness of each individual.

Closing

If space allows, have children sit on the floor in a circle with their feet touching in the center. Tell them to pretend they are slices of pie. Ask them what kind of pie they are. Again emphasize that all can be different and still be "yummy."

Session #7

Happy Moments

Discussion

Acknowledge that their families have been through difficult times having a parent go to jail. Make the point that it is OK for them to be happy even though something unhappy has happened in their life.

Ask them to think about a happy time they remember having before their loved one went to jail, or a happy time they have had since the person has been gone.

Drawing

Have them draw pictures in their booklet of these times.

Share aloud with the group.

Closing

Ahead of time, make an autograph book for each child in the group. Copy the cover on colored paper and staple a few sheets of plain white paper inside, or use a book binding machine to make spiral binder. Give these out and let the children take a few minutes to sign each other's books. They may want to draw pictures of each group friend in their book.

My Autograph Book

We Are Special Friends

Session #8

Popcorn Party

Celebration

Prepare popcorn and drinks for children. Sometimes I play music or show a short cartoon video while students eat.

Evaluation

Ask each group member to share "What I have learned in group" or have them fill out a simple evaluation form.

Give them success cards and scribble booklets to take home.

Closing

Group hug or "jelly roll." (Students hold hands in a line and roll up into a "jelly roll". Leader is in middle and controls the tightness of the hug.)

Resources & References

Gaudin, J. M. Jr. & Sutphen, R. (1993). Foster care vs. extended family care for children of incarcerated mothers. *Journal of Offender Rehabilitation: 19.* 129-147.

Heegaard, M. E. (1995). *The Facilitator's Guide to Drawing Out Feelings.* MN: Woodland Press.

Landy, L. (1984). *Child Support Through Small Group Counseling.* Charlotte, NC: KIDSRIGHTS.

Leon, A. (2000). *Counseling Children Who Have Experienced Extreme Stressors.* Washington, DC: Paper presented at the National Research Conference of Head Start.

Mumola, C. J. (2000). *Incarcerated parents and their children.* Washington, DC: Bureau of Justice Statistics Special Report.

Seymour, C. B. (1998). *Parents in prison: Child welfare policy, program and practice issues.* Washington, DC: Child Welfare League of America.

Simmons, C. W. (2000). *Children of incarcerated parents.* California Research Bureau Note, 7 (n.2).